Teacher's Notes

Beethoven Lives Upstairs

Based on the original work
by Barbara Nichol

Teacher's Notes written
by Susan Hammond

To Sarah and Katie,
who inspired this series

Published by The Children's Group Inc.
1400 Bayly Street, Suite 7
Pickering, Ontario, Canada L1W 3R2
For a complete catalogue, please call 1-800-757-8372
or e-mail moreinfo@childrensgroup.com
Visit us online at http://www.childrensgroup.com
© Classical Kids 1989 Beethoven Lives Upstairs, Original version
© Classical Kids 1998 Beethoven Lives Upstairs, Revised version

Printed in Canada

CONTENTS

LETTER TO TEACHERS

"MONDAY, MARCH 26, 1827. The north wind blows and snow billows through the air. Thunder claps above the empty streets. It is a day that will go down in history."

The stage is now set for the award-winning Classical Kids production, *Beethoven Lives Upstairs*. Since its release, it has captured the hearts of children, adults, teachers and critics through its touching perspective of a lonely young boy's relationship with the composer.

"Why Beethoven?" asks Leonard Bernstein in the *Joy of Music*. What is it about his music that changed the course of music history and demanded that all who followed come to terms with it? Perhaps the word "nobility" best captures that quality that has made the "Ode to Joy" a world anthem, played at the demise of the Berlin Wall, the handover of Hong Kong to China, the Olympics and all those images that move us in times of disaster. In the words of our young Christoph:

"Mr. Beethoven wanted to change the world with his music. Maybe he will, bit by bit..."

Why Beethoven? Because behind the music is a heroic figure struggling with the loss of his most critical faculty: his hearing. Indeed, there is no more poignant image in all of classical music than Beethoven continuing to conduct his last symphony long after the notes had ended. Again Christoph sums up this shattering but inspiring moment with his words:

"To think that he heard all this in his head!"

Why Beethoven? Because children love eccentrics who have the courage to break all the rules. They delight at the stories of Beethoven pouring water over his head in the middle of a room, or standing naked before an open window. They cheer at his defiant outburst:

"There are many princes, but there is only *one* Beethoven!"

Whether you have an extensive background in music or none at all, in these Teacher's Notes you will find more than 70 suggestions ranging broadly across the integrated curriculum: personal biography, social history, geography, science, creative writing, drama, dance, art and music. Here, your library research is collected in one place, along with many classroom activity ideas.

Classical Kids recordings begin with careful research into the music and life of the featured composer. Then we introduce a fictional child into the drama so young listeners have a point of entry into the story. This emotional involvement is primary for allowing them to empathize with the composer, for where the heart goes the mind will follow.

Many teachers have concerns about using audio productions in the classroom where the "fidget factor" cannot be tamed by "things to look at." Yet listening to recordings in class, like reading aloud, can encourage children to create whole worlds in their imaginations. This creative listening is one of childhood's greatest gifts, and is an essential skill for later life.

Let us give our children a window on earlier times, accompanied by glorious music, enticing drama and some profound themes.

Susan Hammond

HOW THIS BOOK IS ORGANIZED

Classical Kids recordings have been used in K–9 classes, but are most suitable for Grades K to 6. We have ranked the activities according to grade level with the symbols below. The icon applies to all the activities in the section, unless otherwise indicated. In the Exploring the Music sections, the icon also includes a number indicating the appropriate National Standard for Arts Education (see page 5).

 K–2   3–4   5–6   3–6   All

Presenting the Recording

This recording can be presented in its entirety (approximately 45 minutes), in two halves or in the six scenes outlined here. Each scene is identified in terms of tape time elapsed, CD track numbers and beginning and ending dialogue. You will find in these Teacher's Notes:

Getting ready: Questions and activities for use before the recording

Scene-by-scene suggestions: For use during the recording
  • The story
  • Music used in the scene
  • Interesting background facts
  • Discussion and activity suggestions
  • Suggestions for exploring the music

Follow-up: Questions and activities for use after the recording
  • Charts: Themes and skills, and a 10-day lesson plan
  • Student's worksheet

Music in the Integrated Curriculum

Although Classical Kids recordings can be enjoyed as musical stories, our aim is to move children from being passive listeners to active participants: to engage their imaginations, to offer new skills and knowledge, to stimulate higher-order thinking skills and, finally, to give every teacher the tools to build a rich learning environment. These Teacher's Notes present more than 70 facts and thought-provoking questions to move beyond music into an integrated curriculum of social studies, creative writing, math, sciences and the other arts.

Our intent is to provide both specialists and general classroom teachers with engaging materials that expand their students' knowledge of music and times past. Instead of presenting a basal text of sequential musical skills, Classical Kids urges teachers and their students to "play with" musical concepts, to develop an interpretive vocabulary, to sing or play classical melodies on simple classroom instruments, to write lyrics, even to venture into composition. Children find it difficult to work in a vacuum, so let these recordings serve as a model, captivating young listeners with a moving story and then motivating them to acquire new facts and skills. Put these recordings in your classroom library for repeated listening.

Classical Kids and Children with Special Needs

Classical Kids recordings do not talk down to children. Our challenge here has been to design concrete activities that are sufficiently broadly based to inspire and involve children with special needs.

Teachers of children with learning disabilities often use the activities designed for younger classes, or allow more time for tasks: retell the story, dance, draw, sing or clap. Those teaching children with physical disabilities concentrate on singing, storyboarding, drawing or discussing events from the past. Teachers of children who are deaf or hard of hearing can tell the compelling story of Beethoven's triumph over deafness in *Beethoven Lives Upstairs*.

ESL students benefit from recordings that use well-spoken English to promote oral comprehension. Singing and writing lyrics are also wonderful ways to learn a second language. Classical Kids materials are available in other languages. Illustrated books of *Beethoven Lives Upstairs* and *Tchaikovsky Discovers America* are available in Spanish, and recordings of *Beethoven Lives Upstairs* and *Vivaldi's Ring of Mystery* are available in French.

The Teacher's Notes in this series encourage gifted students to write variations, study rondo structure, venture into European history and write time-travel stories with shifting points of view.

To all students, we encourage you to ask: "Who would want to do the possible all your life? The *impossible* — that's exciting!"

Assessment

Assessment in the arts is always difficult, often subjective, yet ultimately essential to spur excellence. Depending on what you hope to achieve with your arts program, you can test students individually or in groups, orally or on paper, for skills or understandings. These Notes encourage children to form their own questions, define tasks, discover research strategies, justify interpretations and then create a final product. Each of these stages can be assessed by the teacher. A sample student worksheet is included at the end of this book.

Observe and assess your students not only on final results but also on the care taken with the process. We encourage specialists to move beyond traditional music skills into cultural history, creative writing, research projects, time lines, story boards, set designs, murals or dance. Conversely, general classroom teachers are urged to try musical activities not necessarily based on playing proficiency. These listening and interpretive skills are important for music and for life in general.

Exploring the Music with Classical Kids

The suggested activities in the Exploring the Music sections are coded by number to reflect how they fulfill the U.S. National Standards for Arts Education.

1. *Singing, alone and with others, a varied repertoire of music.* Classical Kids believes that singing is primary for all music-making. The series offers more than 40 classical songs written out, and students are encouraged to write their own lyrics to well-known orchestral pieces and sing them.
2. *Performing on instruments, alone and with others, a varied repertoire.* These Teacher's Notes offer more than 50 pieces written out for recorders, glockenspiels, piano or guitar.

3. *Improvising melodies, variations and accompaniments.* The series encourages actively "playing with" musical elements, making answering phrases in ABA form, creating melodies based on chords and scales, and improvising variations or canons.

4. *Composing and arranging music within specified guidelines.* Be it creating "music from Neptune," writing ragtime, superimposing melodies, or composing music over which to read script, we seek to fire a child's musical imagination.

5. *Reading and notating music.* All the written-out pieces can be photocopied for classroom reading. Some titles include step-by-step descriptions for learning to read notation.

6. *Listening to, analyzing and describing music.* Musical terminology, instrumentation and form are explained. We encourage students to graph the "musical spine" of scenes in terms of tempo, instrumentation and mood. Classical Kids is particularly interested in helping students develop a descriptive vocabulary to interpret and listen to music imaginatively.

7. *Evaluating music and music performances.* All the music on the recordings has been expressly recorded to reflect images in the script. This provides an opportunity to talk about the performances and compare them to other recordings of the same piece.

8. *Understanding relationships between music and the other arts as well as disciplines outside the arts.* Classical Kids offers something unique for the last two criteria (8 and 9). The Discussion and Activities sections link music to other arts and subjects.

9. *Understanding music in relation to history and culture.* In the Background section of every scene, the music is set in its historical context. You will find a wealth of anecdotal facts and vivid descriptions of the times, without having to go to a library for outside sources.

(Adapted from National Standards for Arts Education *published by Music Educators National Conference. Copyright 1994. Reproduced with permission. The complete National Standards and additional materials related to the standards are available from Music Educators National Conference, 1806 Robert Fulton Drive, Reston, VA 22091.)*

Synopsis of the Story

The story of *Beethoven Lives Upstairs* begins with Beethoven's majestic funeral in Vienna. This is followed by a lively exchange of letters between young Christoph and his uncle, a student of music in Salzburg, Austria. Beethoven has moved in upstairs, and the boy pours out his outrage at the true-life eccentricities of this new boarder... hammering on his piano all night, pouring water over his head in the heat of inspiration, fighting with the housekeepers. Through it all, Christoph comes to understand the real Beethoven: his love of nature, the tragedy of his deafness and the greatness of his music. The story ends with Christoph attending the famous first performance of the Ninth Symphony. Eventually, the boy's life returns to normal, but with the touching realization that, "Mr. Beethoven wanted to change the world with his music. Maybe he will do it, bit by bit."

Things to Talk About Before the Recording

Here is how one teacher introduced *Beethoven Lives Upstairs* to his class.

Teacher:	What is a rock star?
Students:	Someone who has wild hair? Yes... Someone who plays really loud? Yes... Someone who makes everyone angry? Yes... Someone who thinks he or she is a god? Yes...
Teacher:	There you have it — Ludwig van Beethoven!

- Play the famous opening of Beethoven's Symphony No. 5. Have your students ever heard it? How would they express the similarities or differences between classical music and pop music?
- Beethoven has long been admired by popular culture. Bring in a *Peanuts* comic book or watch some of Disney's movie *Fantasia* to appreciate how Beethoven has crossed into our 20th-century world.
- Talk about the word "eccentric." Ask if anyone has a neighbor or family friend whom they would call eccentric? Beethoven had a chaotic daily life. He fired servants abruptly, threw food at waiters and sang wildly while walking in the streets.
- Ask if students know anyone who is deaf or hard of hearing? How can people communicate with them?
- Children often ask whether it is possible for a musician to be deaf. Explain how it is possible to hear the music *inside* one's head.
- Beethoven was tormented by music late into the night. Ask if students have had a favorite tune they could not "get out of their head" while they were trying to sleep?
- "There are many princes, but there is only *one* Beethoven!" Discuss with students what this famous quotation might mean.

Classical Kids

SCENE 1: THE FUNERAL, BEETHOVEN MOVES IN

LENGTH OF SCENE: 4:49   TAPE STARTING POINT: SIDE 1/0:00   CD TRACKS 1–2
BEGINS: *"March 26, 1827"*
ENDS: *"To send Mr. Beethoven away!"*

The Story
Christoph's uncle tells of Beethoven's famous funeral in Vienna. Christoph describes the disruption caused to his home when Beethoven moves into the upstairs apartment.

The Music
• Symphony No. 7, Mvt 2
• Symphony No. 5, Mvt 1

Background Information

Beethoven and the Classical Style
It is often helpful to understand where exactly a composer fits into his era. At Beethoven's birth, Bach had been dead for 20 years, Haydn was 38 and Mozart was 14. These composers of the Classical style were followed shortly by the Romantics: Schubert, Mendelssohn, Chopin, Schumann, Liszt and Wagner. Many were born while Beethoven was in his forties.

The late 18th century is often called the Age of Curiosity. It was a time of questioning everything from philosophy, politics, religion, medicine and science. Musicians who had formerly been considered humble servants of the church or court were raised to god-like status. For the first time, the role of the conductor emerged, as urban society demanded larger concert halls and bigger orchestras. Composers became free spirits who expressed the new Romantic ideals of the individual and nature. The world was now ready for Beethoven!

Beethoven's Funeral
Imagine a funeral that could bring an entire city to a standstill! Beethoven was so famous that at his funeral crowds of nearly 50,000 people filled the streets. Schools were let out, and even the humble candle maker supplied free wax for the church service.

Typical of his tumultuous life, Beethoven died during a storm. Friends report that during a flash of lightning, at 5:15 on the evening of March 26, 1827, the composer raised a proud fist to the skies and fell back dead. This gesture illustrates Beethoven's defiant attitude toward both his own deafness and toward the aristocratic social system in which he lived.

The poet Franz Grillparzer wrote Beethoven's eulogy. His eloquent words describe the tragedy of Beethoven's life:

> *If he withdrew from men, it was because they did not want to climb up to him and he could not descend to them. He dwelt alone, because he found no second self. Yet to the end his heart beat for all men... Thus he was, thus he died, thus will he live till the end of time.*

Fact and Fiction

By 1824, Beethoven was no longer living in princely surroundings. At 54 years of age, he was poor and relatively neglected. It is quite plausible that he would move in above a widow and her young family. Although Christoph and his story are not "real," all the facts about Beethoven are true and documented.

Discussion and Activities

Thunder

- Sound effects are powerful tools for building a scene's mood. Play the opening section again and ask your students to identify all the sound effects they hear. [Answer: thunder, passing carriages, tolling bell, children's laughter.]
- In making this recording, many types of thunder were used to represent Beethoven's absent voice. As an exercise in building vocabulary, make a class list of adjectives for thunder (e.g., thunder cracking overhead, window-rattling explosions, rolling thunder over wide spaces, bouncing thunder down an enclosed street).

Personal Stories

Questions to ask:
- What are Christoph's feelings toward Beethoven during this opening scene?
- Have you ever been fascinated by, but afraid of, someone?
- As we learn, Beethoven moved often. Have you ever moved? Did you like it? What can be done to make moving easier, both physically and emotionally?
- Have you ever attended a funeral? In a creative writing class, be a reporter and write a newspaper article about Beethoven's funeral. Bring the scene alive by including all the details you remember from the recording.

Writing and Drawing

- Although most of *Beethoven Lives Upstairs* takes the form of letters, this production opens with a prologue and closes with an epilogue. Discuss these literary devices and their purpose in this recording. [Answer: prologue establishes an important moment in history and epilogue explains a new personal understanding.]
- The opening scene takes the form of a flashforward to Beethoven's death. Many movies use a flashback or flashforward to catch our attention. Make a class list of books or movies that use this device.
- Suggest that your students add a short prologue to a story they have already written or that you are reading in class. Does it improve the story?
- Ask the children to imagine they are in Vienna 150 years ago. Listen to the opening scene again, and have them use art materials to create their impressions of Beethoven's funeral procession: the carriages, horses, crowds, bell tower and church.

Exploring the Music

Symphony No. 7: A Great Funeral March

Beethoven's hearing was failing when he wrote Symphony No. 7. Eye-witnesses report that he conducted the symphony with bizarre antics, "crouching down at the soft sections and jumping up into the air during the louder passages."

Beethoven's Rhythms

Much of the power of Beethoven's music lies in its distinctive rhythms. Two famous examples are found at the opening of this recording, Symphony No. 7 and Symphony No. 5.

Questions to ask and activities to suggest:
- What is the rhythm of the excerpt from Symphony No. 7? [Answer: LONG-short-short.]
- Clap it, then walk to it like a slow funeral march.
- Continue clapping or walking as you sing "London Bridge is Falling Down" and "Yo-Heave-Ho." Can you think of some other songs that share this rhythm?
- What is the rhythm of Symphony No. 7? [Answer: almost the opposite to Symphony No. 7: short-short-short-LONG.]
- Divide the class into two groups and clap the two rhythms on top of each other, as notated below.

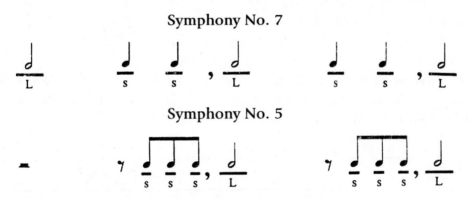

Symphony No. 5: Fate Knocking at the Door

The four opening notes of the Fifth Symphony are probably the most well known in all of musical history. They were often played during World War II to represent "Fate Knocking at the Door" or "Four Notes that Changed the World." This short repeating phrase is called a motif.

- Can your class suggest some adjectives that would account for this designation? [Suggestions: heroic, defiant.]
- As an exercise in understanding musical form, ask your class to write some words for it and sing them each time the motif returns [Suggestions: "You cannot go" or "Beethoven lives."]

Creative Listening

Ask the questions:
- Each instrument in the orchestra has a distinctive "color" to express a certain mood. In this recording, what instrument is used to represent the "injured beast"? [Answer: French horn.]
- How does Beethoven's musical phrase suggest the words "pounding up the stairs above our heads"? [Answer: ascending sequence of notes.]

SCENE 2: LIFE AT CHRISTOPH'S HOUSE

LENGTH OF SCENE: 9:08   TAPE STARTING POINT: SIDE 1/4:49   CD TRACKS 3–5

BEGINS: *"I arrived home last night..."*

ENDS: *"He has been writing with a pencil on the wall!"*

The Story

The uncle reassures Christoph about Beethoven's strange behavior. Everyone in the street is laughing at Beethoven as he stands naked in the window. Christoph begins to sympathize with the loneliness of the composer. More disruption: the housekeeper has stuffed Beethoven's boots with his music! Uncle reminds Christoph about Beethoven's deafness. Christoph describes the view of the river from his father's office. Horrors: Beethoven is pouring water on his head! Christoph thinks Beethoven must be a terrible man if even a prince is afraid him.

The Music
- Piano Sonata, Op. 90, Mvt 2
- Flute Serenade, Op. 23, Mvt 3
- Violin Romance No. 1, Op. 40
- Symphony No. 2, Mvt 4
- "Pathètique" Sonata, Op. 13, Mvt 2
- Contredanse No. 1, in C
- Symphony No. 5, Mvt 2
- Piano Sonata, Op. 14, No. 2, Mvt 2
- Flute Serenade, Op. 23, Mvt 1

Background Information

Listeners often wonder where fiction takes over from fact. These incidents about Beethoven standing naked at the window about his pouring water over his head in a frenzy of writing and about the housekeeper stuffing his boots with his music, are all true and documented.

Dining Out

Here are some incidents about food and restaurants that children might find interesting:
- Beethoven's favorite food was "bread soup," made from pouring gravy over bread and eating the sopping bread with the fingers.
- Beethoven was often so busy composing in restaurants that he sometimes walked out without ordering or paid for a meal he had not eaten.
- Many people who are hard of hearing are disturbed by noise in restaurants. At times, Beethoven became so enraged that he would actually throw his dinner at the waiter.
- Ask if anyone knows an elderly person with this problem. Where would such a person like to sit in a restaurant? [Answer: probably in a corner, to shut out some of extraneous noises and focus the sounds they want to hear.]

Discussion and Activities

Prince Lichnowsky was a loyal friend to Beethoven. He rented out his attic rooms to the young composer when he first came to Vienna. Later, the prince invited Beethoven to take an apartment on his more elegant "piano mobile" (second floor). Beethoven stayed there as a house guest for two years.

Questions to ask:
- Do you like having house guests?
- Are Christoph's feelings toward Beethoven changing? As an exercise in tolerance, discuss strange behavior that makes people uneasy, and how to deal with it.
- Christoph was fascinated with Beethoven because he too was lonely. What do you do when you are lonely?
- When his mother was busy with the twins, Christoph spent his time playing with the stray dog and watching their strange boarder. What do you do when your parents are busy?
- Many children have fears about being laughed at. What advice would you give Christoph to help him solve his problem with Beethoven?
- Try some role-playing between Christoph, Mother, Uncle and Schindler. How would each of these people have a different relationship with, and perspective on, Beethoven?

Beethoven's Raptus

Being alone can help us to be creative. Here is a true story from Beethoven's youth that may touch some of the daydreamers in your class:

> When Beethoven was young, he often visited the von Breuning family in Bonn. They had children about his age and the mother was particularly fond of Beethoven. She never reprimanded her young guest when he seemed to withdraw from the general frenzy of family life into what she called his "raptus." Perhaps she knew that one day he would become a great composer.

Talk with your class about this state of raptus. Ask them:
- How would you describe this mental state?
- Is it similar to daydreaming or something different?
- Are you aware of what you are thinking about, or is it just vague feelings?
- Is there something you like to do after "waking" from this heightened state?

Other Arts

In this section, Christoph describes the disruption and chaos in his house. Divide the class into small groups and explore some of these scenes in writing, drama or dance. For example:
- *Writing.* Like Uncle, children often have a great sensitivity to other people's difficulties. Suggest that your students write to a friend, parent or sibling about how to solve some problem they have perceived.
- *Drama.* Many children will identify with Christoph's misery as he describes the mocking crowd outside his house. Explore those feelings by acting out the humorous naked

conducting scene (except of course the part about getting naked!): Beethoven's antics in the window, young Christoph's fumbling explanations and the comments of the children outside. Is there something to be learned here about creativity and tolerance?

- *Movement.* How is the Contredanse made to sound humorous? [Answer: its bizarre sonority on the synthesizer.] Invent ways to "move like a bear" and "dance like the Viennese ladies."

Exploring the Music

Some of the slow musical excerpts in this scene are particularly lovely. While playing a slow movement from Beethoven, encourage your students to interpret it in their own words. Here are two examples written by nine-year-olds:

As I walk slowly beyond the trees,
My mind slips away like the wind on the breeze.
Not knowing how, or not knowing when,
It just never seems to come back again.　　　　(Natalia)

Silently the stars slip by.
Writing their dreams across the sky.
Nightingales sing out so sweet
As darkness comes to bring us sleep.　　　　(Katie)

This skill of putting into words exactly what we are hearing or feeling is difficult yet important.

- Ask your class whether they think this "Pathètique" movement is "sad." If so, is it sad in the present or in the past? Are the feelings still hurting or have they been resolved? Is there a glow of hope or only deep despair?

Words with Music

Questions to ask:

- In the Flute Serenade, how does the opening flute motif suggest the arrival of the prince? [Answer: sounds like a horn call.] What other two instruments can you identify in this trio? [Answer: violin and viola.]
- How does the Violin Romance bring out the loneliness of Beethoven sitting in his room with a towel around his head? How many violins play the opening phrase? [Answer: one, with playing on two strings at once.]
- How does the music of the river match the words? [Answer: running 16th notes. For those unfamiliar with 16th notes, they are described in the next scene under "Metronome."]
- The image of the river reappears later. For what is a river commonly used as a metaphor? [Answer: life itself.]

- In the Piano Sonata, what captures the ideas of drops of water? [Answer: "staccato," or short chords.]

SCENE 3: VIENNA, BEETHOVEN'S APARTMENT

LENGTH OF SCENE: 11:45   TAPE STARTING POINT: SIDE 1/13:57   CD TRACKS 6–8

BEGINS: *"I've been thinking about your story about the prince."*
ENDS: *"He believes that music can change the world."*

The Story
Uncle tells Christoph about his trip around Vienna. He also describes Beethoven's young life. Christoph describes the bells on Beethoven's desk and the "Dog of Montargis." Uncle reassures Christoph that Beethoven will soon be gone. Christoph describes Beethoven's pianos, his metronome and his thoughts about the composer now that he has gone away for the summer.

The Music
- Polonaise, 21
- *La Marmotte*
- Country Dance in A
- *Für Elise*
- *Flötenuhr*
- Sonatina in G
- Minuet in G
- Violin "Spring" Sonata, Mvt 1
- Écossaise, 83
- Symphony No. 8, Mvt 2
- "Moonlight" Sonata, Op. 27, No. 2, Mvt 1

Background Information

Vienna during the Time of Napoleon
In Beethoven's time, Vienna was a thriving city of 200,000 including an astonishing 6,000 pianists. Home to Haydn, Mozart and Beethoven, this city became the musical capital of the Classical style.

One week before the opening of Beethoven's opera *Fidelio* in 1805, Napoleon's troops marched into the city. With his apartment only blocks from the direct line of shelling, Beethoven would cover his head with pillows to shut out the noise of exploding bombs. He later claimed that the shelling of Vienna by Napoleon actually caused his deafness: "Nothing but drums, cannons and human misery in every form!"

As a fervent supporter of the common people, Beethoven felt deeply betrayed by Napoleon's declaring himself Emperor. He even removed his dedication of Symphony No. 3 to Napoleon, saying: "It is a pity that I do not understand the art of war as well as I do the art of music. I would conquer him!"

Beethoven's Young Life in Bonn

Beethoven's early years were difficult. His father was determined that his son should follow in Mozart's steps and earn money as a child prodigy. Once his father said: "What stupid stuff are you scraping at now? You know I can't stand hearing it! Play the notes in front of you, or all your scrapings will amount to nothing!" He would box the boy's ears violently when he did not practice. Unfortunately, Beethoven's mother was a weak woman who could not defend her son against her volatile husband. As a result, Beethoven preferred his grandfather, who was a court musician at the Elector of Bonn. Wherever he moved in Vienna, Beethoven hung a large framed picture of his grandfather on the wall.

Beethoven was able to attend school only until the age of 11. As a result, he had troubles with addition and multiplication all his life. And yet he could hear thousands of notes in his head!

Beethoven and Mozart

At the age of 17, Beethoven traveled from Bonn to Vienna to study with Mozart. Mozart, 14 years his senior, was most impressed and agreed to teach him, saying: "Watch this young man carefully, for he will one day make a great noise." Unfortunately, Beethoven was called back home to take care of his dying mother. By the time he could return to Vienna, Mozart had died and Beethoven had to study with old Papa Haydn, who was almost 40 years older than he was. It was said at the time that "Beethoven received the spirit of Mozart from the hands of Haydn."

Beethoven's Bells

Beethoven had a lifelong fascination with bells. As a child in Bonn, he had always loved the famous carillon at the Elector's court. When he was just seven, the bell tower collapsed in a mighty fire. On moving to Vienna at 21, Beethoven chose to live between two churches, a pattern he followed his entire life. Perhaps bells were one of the few sounds he could still hear.

On his desk, Beethoven kept a collection of bells as well as a picture made out of his own hair.

On Moving

Beethoven moved a total of 77 times in his life: 33 times within Vienna, and 34 times to various summer lodgings. He would sometimes leave a new apartment after only three weeks!

Although he moved often around Vienna, Beethoven was not a great world traveler. He planned several trips to London, and even wrote some British folk songs, but never crossed the English Channel. The London Philharmonic successfully premiered both his Fifth and Ninth Symphonies. Beethoven had even promised them a Tenth Symphony, which of course was never written. The London Philharmonic held a benefit concert for Beethoven when he was dying.

Discussion and Activities

- The Beethoven household obviously had trouble with his practicing. Ask your students whether this is a problem in their families. How have they solved this problem?

On Uncles

In this production, you meet two uncles. Christoph's uncle actively participates in letter-writing with his nephew. The other uncle is, of course, Beethoven himself. The true story of the composer's nephew, Karl, is a sad one. Karl was a child of about six when his father died. Beethoven spent many difficult years trying to raise Karl and keep him away from his erratic mother, Beethoven's sister. The composer's alternate indulgences and ignoring of the child made life miserable for both of them.

Invite the class to talk about uncles:

- Why is it possible to have uncles or aunts of greatly different ages?
- What is the class opinion on the role of uncles or aunts in today's families?

Creating Your Own Soundscapes

Ask your class whether they like to collect things outdoors. Consider collecting sounds as well. Go on a class expedition to make a "picture in sound" of your city, town or country-side. You can use any inexpensive tape recorder with an internal or external microphone for this project.

- Before going out on your field trip, make a list of sounds you might expect to hear in your area. Then really "listen" to your environment. Be ready for some surprises!
- Some classes might like to include voice-overs. In the style of a newscaster, describe what is happening while you tape your soundscape. Remember that this must be done *at the time of recording* or you will erase your sound effects with the voice-over.

Drama and Mime

The trip around Vienna contains some of Beethoven's lesser-known but charming pieces. These street scenes can be effectively acted out in class using mime. Divide the class into small groups and let the recording "activate" each scene such that as one activity passes by, another begins.

- March to the Polonaise.
- Mime the organ grinder on the corner with his monkey. Crowds can gesticulate, pay money and "comment" on what they are seeing.
- Create a folk dance for Beethoven's *Country Dance*.
- Invent a movement to interpret the famous *Für Elise*.
- Act out the wooden men in the town clock to the *Flötenuhr*.
- Dance a minuet like "The Dog of Montargis," which was a popular traveling show that came to Vienna from France.

Alone in the House

- From what your class now knows about Beethoven, have them make a collage to represent his room: his metronome, his ear trumpets, bells, piano and piles of manuscript paper.
- Ask students to describe their own room and draw a picture or floor plan.

Exploring the Music

Beethoven's Pianos

Beethoven's pianos were famous. At least four were given to him by manufacturers who sought his endorsement, much like sportswear manufacturers give their products to athletes today.

Because the pianos had wooden rather than metal frames, they were more fragile than today's and could support less tension on the strings. As a result, they made far less sound in Beethoven's day than today's pianos.

To compensate for his declining hearing, Beethoven would lie on the floor and hold in his teeth a stick that touched the piano frame. This allowed the sound waves to enter his body through the floorboards and enter his head through his teeth!

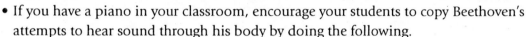

- If you have a piano in your classroom, encourage your students to copy Beethoven's attempts to hear sound through his body by doing the following.
  - Put one end of a pencil or stick in your mouth and rest the other end on the piano frame, while someone else plays.
  - Describe what you feel and hear.

Beethoven's Metronomes

Beethoven often visited a friend named Malzel who was an inventor. This famous "Court Mechanician" made four ear trumpets for Beethoven as well as a "Panharmonium" or mechanical orchestra. Today, Malzel is best known as the inventor of the metronome. Then called a musical chronometer, it had a small lever that was set in motion by a cogwheel. A little hammer then struck a wooden anvil. By 1817, Malzel had replaced the hammer and anvil with the traditional swinging pendulum. Bring in a modern metronome and study this important musician's tool with your class.

There are two purposes for a metronome:

1. To keep an even beat
2. To establish the speed of the beats

How Fast are the Beats?

- Set the metronome at 60 beats per minute. The ticks should match the movement of the seconds hand on your class clock or digital seconds on your watches.
- Listen to the "metronome movement" of the Eighth Symphony as played here. What metronome setting would you use for this piece? [Answer: 100.]
- Check your pulse rate with the metronome. Check your pulse rate after running and notice how the speed of the metronome changes.

- If you are using a pendulum-type of metronome (not electronic), explain in scientific terms why moving the marker down means faster. [Answer: the arc of the swing becomes smaller for each click.]

Subdivide the Beats

Set the metronome at 80. Ask your students to say a word to each click with an increasing number of syllables as below:

- Say the word "one" on each beat (1 syllable)
- Divide the beat into eighths with the word "silly" (2 syllables)
- Divide the beat into triplets with the word "galloping" (3 syllables)
- Divide the beat into 16th notes with "alligator" (4 syllables)
- Combine them all in a rhythmic sentence with one word per click.
- Divide the class into four groups. With each group starting after the word "one," chant "one silly galloping alligator" like a round.

Four Famous Pieces for Piano

1. The Sonatina in G, which underscores the story of Beethoven's childhood, is often studied by young pianists. Can anyone in your class play it? Now ignore the words and listen only to the Sonatina behind them. How many times does the main melody return? [Answer: twice.]

2. *Für Elise*, like the "Ode to Joy," is one of the first classical pieces people try to play on the piano. Beware — it is not as easy as it sounds.

3. Most students in Suzuki courses play the Minuet in G. The nonsense words here are based on "Down by the Bay" and were written by a young class. It is fun to sing and can be accompanied by the glockenspiel as indicated. Can anyone in your class play it on piano or violin? Young children enjoy barking along with the dog on the recording!

4. The "Moonlight" Sonata was so-named many years after Beethoven's death by the poet-critic Ludwig Rellstab. The piece reminded him of moonlight on Lake Lucerne. Can your class think of other images for this tranquil piece? Listen to the entire first movement and decide how to best interpret it: in words, drawing or dance. Alternatively, use this timeless piece to relax and refresh yourselves during a hurried day.

5. The Classical Kids recording *Daydreams and Lullabies* encourages students to speak words over music. While playing a recording of the "Moonlight" Sonata, see how your students instinctively pace their reading of the following letter to this wonderful piece of music. Describe the main ideas or feelings in your own words.

> Dear Uncle,
>
> Spring has come and gone and now it is summer. The house is quiet because Mr. Beethoven has gone to Baden. He has gone to find a house where he will spend the hottest months. He said he will be back tomorrow before lunch.
>
> Tonight, as I write you, it is evening but, of course, I cannot sleep. From my room, I can hear Mother, playing as she used to when I was small.
>
> I have been lying here thinking about something Mr. Schindler said. He said, "Mr. Beethoven works so hard, because he believes that music can change the world."

Minuet in G

Arr. Susan Hammond

SCENE 4: A STORM, A PARTY, PRINCES AND DEAFNESS

LENGTH OF SCENE: 10:07   TAPE STARTING POINT: SIDE 2/0:00   CD TRACKS 9–12

BEGINS: *"Do you wonder where Mr. Beethoven goes..."*
ENDS: *"Slowly, Mr. Beethoven was going deaf."*

The Story

Christoph teases his baby sister, then is sent off to get pencils for Mr. Beethoven. When he returns, the composer takes him for a walk in the country. A storm erupts. There is a noisy party upstairs as Beethoven prepares for the final concert. Christoph and his mother listen to a soprano singing an Italian song upstairs. The uncle tells Christoph about Beethoven's early years as a pianist, his treatment of the aristocracy and the composer's deafness.

The Music

- Flute Serenade, Mvt 2
- Symphony No. 6, "Storm"
- "Nel Cor Più" Variations
- Concerto No. 1 in C, Mvt 1
- Concerto No. 5 in E Flat, "The Emperor," Mvt 2

Background Information

Beethoven the Romantic

Like the Romantic composers who followed him, Beethoven loved nature in a very special way. He would often rise early at 5 a.m. and walk all day in the country for inspiration. Oblivious to weather, he would return with his music notebooks stained with water. It was sometimes said that "Beethoven loves a tree better than any man."

Beethoven firmly believed that an individual artist was greater than any royalty who employed him. When the Empress of Austria passed in the streets, Beethoven alone refused to bow. Even when visiting Viennese palaces, he refused to give up his gruff peasant ways. He rebelled against the strict social rules that demanded that dinner be served at precisely 3 p.m., that guests be invited by printed invitation only, that they announce themselves with a specific number of bell-rings (three for a prince and two for a count), that their numbers were regulated according to the function. One never invited 13 guests!

Beethoven's patrons had a clever way of encouraging him to perform at their parties. They would occupy all the chairs except the piano stool, knowing the composer could not resist running his hands over the keyboard. If music paper was left casually on the piano, a new piece might even be born before their very eyes!

Beethoven's Deafness

At 28, Beethoven began to hear humming and buzzing in his ears. By his late forties, he was totally deaf. To understand the progress of his disease, read aloud this letter, which he wrote in 1804.

> Let me tell you that my most prized possession, my hearing, has greatly deteriorated... The symptoms are said to be caused by the condition of my abdomen... When I am playing and composing, my affliction still hampers me least; it affects me most when I am in company... my ears continue to hum and buzz day and night. I must confess that I lead a miserable life. For almost two years, I have ceased to attend any social functions, just because I find it impossible to say to people: I am deaf. If I had any other profession I might be able to cope with my infirmity; but in my profession it is a terrible handicap... At a distance I cannot hear the high notes of instruments or voices... I can hear sounds, it is true, but cannot make out the words. But if anyone shouts, I can't bear it!

Beethoven's doctors tried many cures. They poured milk and ground nuts into his ears. They rubbed ointment on his arms to produce blisters that might drain any infection. None worked, and Beethoven continued to seek help for his malady right up to two weeks before his death. Medical experts now say that his deafness was more likely due to damaged nerve endings than to any external causes.

Discussion and Activities

Questions to ask:
- Halfway through this recording, can you see a change in the relationship between Christoph and Beethoven?
- It is reported that Beethoven would wait out a storm under a tree. Have you ever been caught in a big storm? What happened? Is this a good strategy?
- What do you do during grown-up parties at your house? What does the rest of your family do during your parties?
- Beethoven had great courage to continue composing while he was deaf. How do you define courage? Discuss other examples of courage shown by someone with a disability. In what way can a disability sometimes be seen as an opportunity?
- Any artist lives a rich inner life. Talk about imagination. Is everyone's imagination different or are there common themes? How do you think your imagination differs from your family or friends?

More Sound Effects

In both audio and video productions, sound effects are essential for creating a sense of place.
- Ask your class to list the sound effects they hear in the party scene. Imagine they are creating the sound for a film that includes a child's party. What effects would they add into the mix? [Suggestions: "Happy Birthday" song, running, cutlery noises, clapping, laughing, crying.]
- Try to find a book on how to make sound effects. Experiment with the ones below or make up some new ones. Record them if you can, and see if a friend can guess what they are. Examples:

- Imitate the sounds of animals (with your voice).
- Make the sound of the wind (using your voice, a fan, or swinging a plastic tube).
- Do you know how movies make the sound of a punch in the face? [Answer: hitting a piece of meat with a hammer.]
- Water drops can be dry! How could such a sound be created? [Answer: tap your finger gently on a plastic bowl.]

Exploring the Music

The Sixth Symphony

The year 1808 was a productive one for Beethoven. At the age of 38, he wrote both the Fifth and Sixth Symphonies, two works that mark the turn from Classical to Romantic music. Coincidentally, Josef Haydn, the founder of the Classical style, died in that same year.

Probably the greatest musical depiction of a storm is found in Beethoven's Sixth Symphony. Suggest that your class:

- Listen to this "Storm" movement and put into words how Beethoven captures a storm in music. [Answer: rushing violin scales, screaming piccolos, swirling motifs.]
- Find or make some instruments and noise-makers to build up a storm in your class- room, including wind, rain and thunder. Divide the class in two groups; while one group adds effects into the Beethoven's music, the other can interpret the storm in dance.
- Watch Disney's *Fantasia* to see how a cartoon-maker interpreted the Sixth Symphony.

"Nel Cor Più": Singing and Playing

Beethoven often wrote variations on popular songs such as "Rule Britannia" and "God Save the Queen." These variations on "Nel Cor Più," from Paisello's opera *La Molinara*, are often played by young pianists today. Beethoven slipped them under the door of a young lady who had attended the opera with him and wanted a piano rendition.

Recorders. This two-recorder version is simple to play because it moves within a range of only six notes.

Singing. Children often find the operatic singing on this recording funny. Singing tech- nique is a complicated subject that deserves more space than is offered here. However, see if your students can develop their singing voices by experimenting with this these vocal techniques on the nursery song "Hot Cross Buns":

- Sing "Hot Cross Buns" as you would around a campfire.
- Now shout-sing it as you might at a baseball game.
- Concentrate on your breathing. Take a large, deep diaphragm breath from the front of the body and sing in a "breathy" way, somewhat in the style of a bar-singer. Notice how you can also expand the back of your rib cage to get even more air.
- Raise the pitch. You will notice a change in your singing technique, simply because other techniques are impossible at this higher pitch.

- Now focus the sound in your head and avoid expelling all the air at once. Drop your jaw to create a vertical, not horizontal face, and sing a single note on the "ah" of "hot" and "cross."
- Try singing the entire song with this focused head tone.
- Children are great imitators. Listen to the recording and imitate the singer's sound — you might get surprising results.
- From the singer's expression on the recording, see if the class can guess what the song "Nel Cor Più" is about. [Answer: a woman flirting with a man.]
- What language is the singer using? [Answer: Italian.]
- Write some lyrics and sing this song to make it truly yours!

Nel Cor Più

arr. Sue Hammond

"Nel Cor Più": Composing Variations

- Explore Beethoven's variation techniques by having students write their own variations on "Three Blind Mice."

Three   blind   mice.

- Change the rhythm and repeat some notes.

Three   blind   mice.

- Add extra notes to wrap around the melody.

Three   blind   mice.

- Add an Orff accompaniment below or above the melody: G's and D's.
- Sing it in a minor key.
- Try some syncopated rhythms.
- Speed it up or slow it down.
- Sing it as a round.
- Turn the tune upside down: when the note go up, you go down.
- Change the dynamics from loud to soft.

Piano Concerto No. 5: "The Emperor"

The deafness scene in *Beethoven Lives Upstairs* features one of Beethoven's most haunting melodies, the Adagio from the "Emperor" Concerto (again, this is not the name Beethoven gave to the piece). Today, many movies use its noble beauty to express moments of tremendous feeling.

- Listen to the entire movement on another recording and compare it to this version. Ask your students: Is it faster? Is it slower? Is the piano more or less prominent?
- Have students use art materials to show what this music suggests to them.
- Ask your students to describe an experience they might have had in their life that this music would express.

SCENE 5: THE NINTH SYMPHONY

LENGTH OF SCENE: 8:03   TAPE STARTING POINT: SIDE 2/10:07   CD TRACKS 13–14

BEGINS: *"How much happier you sound."*

ENDS: *"Up there on the stage, Mr. Beethoven bowed and bowed again."*

The Story

Rehearsals are not going well. Christoph describes the excited mood at home. A soprano gives him tickets to the Ninth Symphony. Christoph worries about ruining everything when he accidentally knocks Mr. Beethoven's papers on the floor. As the "Ode to Joy" begins, Uncle reassures Christoph that Beethoven is not angry. The quiet night before the concert is full of anticipation for the Ninth Symphony.

The Music

- Bass excerpts from Symphony No. 9
- Violin "Spring" Sonata, Mvt 4
- "Rage over a Lost Penny"
- Symphony No. 9, Mvt 4, "Ode to Joy"

Background Information

Beethoven's Last Symphony

When Beethoven was writing the Ninth Symphony, his enterprising landlord in Baden insisted that new window shutters be installed. In a previous summer, Beethoven had covered them with musical notations and the landlord sold them to tourists for a good fee!

The words to the "Ode to Joy" were written by Friedrich Schiller. Because they concerned subjects dear to his heart — nature, brotherhood and the joy of music — Beethoven had wanted to set this poem to music since he was 21. Thus, in the last movement of his last symphony, Beethoven fulfilled his lifelong goal.

The first performance of the Ninth Symphony was agony for the musicians. The basses, long used to thumping out rhythms in the back of the orchestra, were now being asked to become soloists like today's instrumentalists. In addition, several amateur orchestras and choirs worked separately, then were brought together for this historic occasion: the first-ever symphony to include a choir.

Nonetheless, the Ninth Symphony was a huge success. Audiences gasped at the timpani outburst in the Scherzo. The second movement was often interrupted by applause. Beethoven let another conductor conduct, but anxiously checked the tempos from beside him. Surely the most poignant moment in musical history is Beethoven's continuing to beat time after his symphony was over. Only when the soprano turned him to face the exultant crowd did Vienna realize that their hero was completely deaf!

Discussion and Activities

Embarrassing Moments

This incident about Beethoven counting out 60 coffee beans for every cup is true. Ask your students whether they have habits or superstitious rituals they use when they are nervous.

Children often have the terrible feeling of having "ruined" an adult's work or treasured object through their own clumsiness or inexperience. This is certainly Christoph's feeling at dropping the music pages.

- Invite the children to describe some of their embarrassing moments and how they were resolved. Do the feelings live on?
- Sometimes when we are acutely embarrassed, our sense of hearing is affected. Ask these questions:
  - Why do you think you cannot hear what is being said? [Suggestion: your attention is on yourself.]
  - Why can even the smallest sound seem huge? [Suggestion: every nerve ending is raw.]
  - What are some other symptoms of nervousness or embarrassment? [Suggestions: sweaty palms, "butterflies in the stomach."]
  - How is nervousness like, or unlike, fear?

Beethoven's Conversation Books

Beethoven often conversed with friends by writing in his conversation books.

- Divide the class into pairs and have the children write down everything they want to say to their partner for five minutes. After this exercise, discuss:
  - How does writing down everything change the things you talk about?
  - Do you feel like a different kind of person on paper?
  - How is this like, or unlike, conversing in a foreign language?
  - How is this like, or unlike, chatting on-line today?
  - Do you find this method of talking exhausting?

Exploring the Music

The Ode to Joy: Music Appreciation

Beethoven builds his "Ode to Joy" very slowly. To appreciate this magnificent piece fully, listen to a recording of the entire last movement of the Ninth Symphony. Notice how Beethoven first introduces the melody far down in the cellos and basses and then moves it up into the higher strings. With each repetition of the "Ode to Joy," another layer of sound is added.

Questions to ask:

- Listen to the inner melody that lies underneath the main theme. Which woodwind plays it? [Answer: bassoon.]
- How many repeated chords do you find at the end of the movement? [Answer: 32.]
- What kind of movement does the final section suggest? Try galloping to it.

Performing the "Ode to Joy"

Beethoven's "Ode to Joy" is often the first piece a child learns to play. Its melody has a noble simplicity that engraves itself on our minds.

- Look at the piece written out here and notice how, with a few exceptions, each note moves step by step. This makes it very easy to play on recorders or beginning strings. More advanced classes should add the accompaniment written here.

- The "Ode to Joy" is also easy to sing. Sing it using this this translation of Schiller, or the "Alphabet Song" as written below. Then write your own lyrics.

<table>
<tr><td>

Ode to Joy

Praise and joy, immortal gladness,
Gift to man eternally.
We give thanks for joy unbounding,
Celebrate life's harmony.

Music's magic boldly sounding,
Bring together friends and foe.
All untie us truly brothers,
Sing together, lustrous glow.

</td><td>

Alphabet Song

Let me sing my A-B-C's,
As Beethoven has taught me.
A-B-C-D, E-F-Gee,
H-J-K-L, LMNOP.

Q-R-S-T, U and Vee,
W-oo and X-Y-Z.
Now I've sung my A-B-C's,
Next time won't you sing with me.

</td></tr>
</table>

Composing

As stated above, the "Ode to Joy" is based on the first five notes of the scale. Here is an easy exercise in composition:

- Begin on any note and sing a phrase to your class using only next-door notes (that is, the next note on the scale).
- Now have your students sing "an answering phrase," again using only adjacent notes. Here are some examples of children's responses:

Teacher sings:

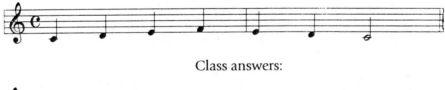

Class answers:

Did you know that you can sing the "Alphabet Song" using almost any nursery rhyme?

- For example, sing the "words" to the "Alphabet Song" to "London Bridge is Falling Down." These songs all have similar structures of four-bar phrases, with four beats each, often in an ABA pattern.
- Try to write an original melody using the words to the "Alphabet Song" using this nursery rhyme structure of four balanced phrases.

Ode to Joy

For 2 recorders

Arr. Susan Hammond

SCENE 6: EPILOGUE: A FINAL UNDERSTANDING

LENGTH OF SCENE: 2:45   TAPE STARTING POINT: SIDE 2/18:10   CD TRACKS 15–16

BEGINS: *"As you know, Mr. Beethoven moved away."*
ENDS: *"Mr. Beethoven wanted to change the world with his music. Maybe he will do it... bit by bit."*

The Story

Christoph reports on meeting Beethoven in the street. He describes how both of their lives have changed since the composer moved away. Christoph can now keep the dog, and has named him Metronome, "because of his wagging tail!" Years later, Uncle finds a letter from Christoph and is pleased that the boy has finally come to understand his experiences when Beethoven lived upstairs.

The Music

- Sonata, Op. 49, No. 2, Mvt 2
- Symphony No. 6, "Shepherd's Theme"

Background Information

The events of this recording occurred around 1824. Beethoven's last years were ones of increasing sickness, poverty and public neglect. After this last symphony, Beethoven turned to writing more sparse musical forms such as string quartets.

Beethoven caught pneumonia while returning to Vienna from his brother's estate. Although it was a cold rainy night, his wealthy brother refused him the use of his closed carriage. On reaching Vienna, Beethoven pleaded with his nephew Karl to fetch a doctor. Instead, Karl chose to go drinking, leaving his uncle desperately sick in bed. A few weeks later, Beethoven died of pneumonia and dropsy. Because of this story, some say that Beethoven's family actually caused his death.

Discussion and Activities

Questions to ask:
- How has Christoph's attitude toward Beethoven changed throughout the recording?
- How have Beethoven's feelings changed toward Christoph?
- How do we know this? [Answer: for the first time, we hear of a direct conversation between the two and of physical contact.]
- What were some of their earlier encounters? [Answer: the trip to the country, the giving of tickets, the shoulder squeeze in the hall.]
- Children often have "crushes" on adults whom they greatly admire. The smallest attention becomes very important. Do you have some important adults in your life outside of your immediate family?
- When did we last hear about the river? [Answer: in reference to Christoph's father and his office.]
- Do you have a place you like to visit when you want to think about something important?

- What has the river come to symbolize in the recording? [Answer: a place of reflection, a symbol of growing up.] Talk about the river as a metaphor for life in movies such as *A River Runs Through It.*
- What does the dog moving in mean to Christoph? [Answer: his grieving over his father is over, his mother is ready to let him take on more responsibilities.]

Creative Writing

- Review your discussion about prologues and epilogues from Scene 1. Ask your students to add an epilogue to a story they have already written. The content could include what happened years later, or what lessons were learned.
- Be sure to end this recording with an exercise in letter writing. Here are some examples of letters written by students with learning disabilities (spelling intact!). It is encouraging to see the profound sympathy expressed for Beethoven and the number of facts about his life that have been remembered.

March 3, 1824
Dear Mr. Beethoven,
I have been having a hard time with you getting up at night and playing your music. I never get any sleep. It is nice music, but I am Fed up. The babies wake up and I don't get any sleep.
From Chrisoph

March 3, 1824
Dear Mr. Beethoven,
Can you stop all that racket now please? I know that you have a hard time understanding what I am trying to tell you when I am speaking. That's why I am writing to you.
From Christoph

Dear Mr. Beethoven,
I am sorry you are deaf.
I like your music.
I am sorry you are dead.
From Christoff

March 3, 1824
Dear Mr. Beethoven,
Can you stop writing on the walls? Why do you dump water over your head? It's ruinning my floors. I have been hating when you wake up the babies. I know you can't hear but you're so loud. If there where special thing to put in your ears, I would get them for you.
From Christoph

March 3, 1824
Dear Mr. Beethoven,
I hope you like your new house. Bye the way, could you quiet your music down? Would you sop stomping on the stares?. Would you stop being loud in the morning. If all these things you would do, that wud be good.
From Christoph

March 3, 1824
Dear Mr. Beethoven,
I think you are inside a very nice man. Sometimes I get frusteratted. But I understand that you are deaf.
From Christophe

Dear Mr. Beethoven
I love your music. I'm sorry you are deaf. Do you have glasses? You must like music because you go to restaurants and you order. They make the food and you go home and play music instead of eating.
From Cristoph

Exploring the Music

A Study in Sonority

Classical Kids recordings try to juxtapose different sonorities to dispel the frequent assertion that "all classical music sounds the same." Here a simple piano piece "freshens the ears" after the mighty Ninth Symphony and before the warm Sixth Symphony, which ends the recording.

- As a class activity, listen again to the entire recording and make a chart of its music in terms of instrumentation, tempo and mood. Here is a beginning:

MUSIC	INSTRUMENTATION	TEMPO	MOOD
Symphony No. 7, Mvt 2	Full orchestra	Slow	Solemn, dignified
Symphony No. 5, Mvt 1	Full orchestra	Fast	Exciting, assertive
Sonata, Op. 90, Mvt 2	Piano	Moderate	Warm, simple
Serenade, Op. 23, Mvt 3	Flute, violin, viola	Moderate–fast	Royal, rippling
Romance No. 1, Op. 40	Violin, orchestra	Slow	Lonely, rich

The "Shepherd's Theme"

The "Shepherd's Theme" of the Sixth Symphony warmly illuminates the epilogue to *Beethoven Lives Upstairs*. Whereas the "Ode to Joy" is based on a scale, the "Shepherd's Theme" is based on a four-note chord. Its first 10 notes never leave the home chord of F major!

- Any melody is best recalled by singing it. Even the youngest students enjoy singing this "Shepherd's Theme" to these simple words about nature.

Early one morning,　　　　　　　*Later that evening*
I heard the robin sing,　　　　　*I heard the loon's call,*
His song seemed to tell me　　　*His song seemed to tell me*
That soon it would be spring.　　*That soon it would be fall.*

- Alternatively play it on recorders with a single repeated glockenspiel note on C.

After the Recording

Questions to ask and activities to suggest:

- Why were letters used on this production? Answers include:
  - Letters can use a more formal, artistic language.
  - Monologue is less distracting than dialogue over music.
  - People can often express feelings in writing more easily than talking directly to somebody.
  - Given Beethoven's deafness, it is hard to imagine how his voice might have sounded.
  - Children love to write and receive letters.
  - Christoph's letters can give us a child's point of view.
- Write a new story, or rewrite an old one, using letters exchanged between two characters.
- Be a reporter for the school newspaper and interview Beethoven to learn more about his troubles and his music.
- Tell the story of *Beethoven Lives Upstairs* in your own words.

- List your five favorite sections. Compare choices and discuss your reasons for them.

Shepherd's Theme

Arr. Susan Hammond

- Write in a diary or journal how you feel about Beethoven or this recording.
- Which music did you like best? Take recordings out of the library and listen to some entire pieces. Think about what you see in your mind's eye as you listen to this music.

- Attend a local concert or write to a radio station and request some of Beethoven's music. Invite a musician into your school to play for your class and talk about how this music differs from that of other composers. Remember that even a music student from a nearby conservatory or university can be one of your most valuable assets!
- Research more about Beethoven's life and make a class project about this famous classical composer. Investigate the relationship between Beethoven, Mozart, Haydn and Schubert.

- Consider creating a school production based on *Beethoven Lives Upstairs*. Here are some ideas:
  - Rewrite the script in dialogue rather than letter form. Try using contemporary language.
  - Rewrite the play, telling the adventures of having a rock musician boarding upstairs.

Students who enjoyed listening this recording will enjoy the video version of Beethoven Lives Upstairs. *A live-action film shot in Prague, the capital of the Czech Republic, it gives a vivid impression of Beethoven and old Europe. The story is also available in book form in English and Spanish, and there is an interactive CD-ROM for children to use on their own.* Beethoven Lives Upstairs *can be booked as a school or symphony show.*

CLASSICAL KIDS AND THE INTEGRATED CURRICULUM

This chart and the following 10-day Lesson Plan illustrate the themes and skills developed in these Teacher's Notes for *Beethoven Lives Upstairs*. The page numbers of each activity are noted in the 10-day chart.

There is also a sample question sheet after the Lesson Plan for those teachers wishing to assess their students' skills and knowledge with a short test.

Core Area	Beethoven
Time Frame	1770–1827
Geography	Austria
Social Studies	• Napoleon • Age of Curiosity • Vienna
Creative Writing	• Writing letters • Reading to music • Character development • Prologues and epilogues • Retelling story • Fact and fiction • Interviews
Modern Issues	• Embarrassment • Disabilities • Loneliness • Imagination • Role playing
Other Arts	• Drawing scenes • Painting to music • Sound effects • Mime and dance • Videos and comics
Music	• Analyzing excerpts • Playing and singing • Composing variations • Motifs and rhythms • Notation • Biography • Sonority and instruments
Math and Science	• Beethoven and math • Malzel: an inventor • Cures for deafness

Suggested Lesson Plan

Week One

MONDAY	TUESDAY	WEDNESDAY	THURSDAY	FRIDAY
Side One • Fact and fiction (9, 13) • Letter writing (30)	**Side Two** • Retelling story (34) • Favorite parts (32) **Modern Issues** • Feelings, fears (9) • Loneliness (12, 21) • Imagination (12, 21) • Embarrassment (12, 26) • Character development (9, 12, 21, 29) • Uncles (16)	**Biography** • Childhood (15) • Mozart (15) • Moving (9, 15) • Dining out (11) • Courage (21) • Deafness (20) • Death (29) • Funeral (8–10) • Conversation books (26) • Research Beethoven's life (32)	**Social Studies** • Age of Curiosity (8) • Napoleon (14) • Nature and the Romantics (20) • Vienna (14)	**Creative Writing** • Prologues and epilogues (11) • Letters (14, 30, 31) • Interviews (31) • Poetry, images (13, 29) • Reading to music (18)

Week Two

MONDAY	TUESDAY	WEDNESDAY	THURSDAY	FRIDAY
Other Arts • Drawing scenes (9, 24) • Role play (12) • Mime, dance (13, 16, 26) • Sound effects (9, 16, 21)	**Video** • Comparison to recording (32) – Character – Setting	**Video cont'd** • *Fantasia* (7) • *Peanuts* (8) • Sonority chart (31) • Worksheet (35)	**Music Appreciation** • Motifs (10) • Instruments (10, 13) • Pianos (17) • "Ode to Joy" (25–28) • Symphonies Nos. 5, 6, 7, 8 (22, 24) • Metronome and rhythm (17)	**Music Making** • Singing (24, 27, 28, 32) • Minuet in G (18, 19) • "Storm" (22) • "Shepherd's Theme" (34) • Reading rhythm (18) • Composition (23, 27) • "Nel Cor Più" (22) • Singing technique (22)

Worksheet for Beethoven Lives Upstairs

1. Beethoven was born in the year _____
   He died in _____ at the age of _____

2. He lived in the city of _____
   in the country of_____

3. His nephew was named _____

4. Was Beethoven married? _____

5. Why is Christoph upset? _____
   _____
   _____

6. Beethoven was seen in his own time as an eccentric. List three scenes where Beethoven shows he is not afraid to be different. _____
   _____
   _____
   _____

7. Tell the story of *Beethoven Lives Upstairs* in your own words._____
   _____
   _____
   _____

8. List three sad scenes. _____
   _____
   _____

9. List three funny scenes. _____
   _____
   _____

10. Who was the Dog of Montargis? _____
    _____
    _____

11. Give two of Beethoven's famous quotations.
    _____
    _____
    _____

12. How do the characters of Beethoven and Christoph change in this recording? _____
    _____
    _____

13. Describe Beethoven's childhood. _____
    _____
    _____
    _____

14. Describe Beethoven's room. _____
    _____
    _____
    _____

15. What did Beethoven have on his desk? ____
    _____

16. Do you think the ending of *Beethoven Lives Upstairs* was happy, sad or both? Why? ____
    _____
    _____

17. What was your favorite part? Why? _____
    _____
    _____

18. What was your favorite piece of music?
    _____
    _____

19. Why do you think the "Moonlight" Sonata was given its name? _____
    _____

20. How many pianos did Beethoven have?
    _____

ANSWERS: Cut off this portion before photocopying worksheet. (1) 1770, 1827, 57; (2) Vienna, Austria; (3) Karl; (4) no; (5) His father has died, he is lonely, and noisy Beethoven has moved in upstairs; (6) He pours water over his head, he sings in the streets, he shouts at his housekeepers; (7) N/A; (8) Beethoven sitting with a towel around his head, Uncle telling of his deafness, Beethoven unable to hear end of Symphony No. 9; (9) Beethoven standing naked in window, barking dog, Beethoven's room; (10) A traveling show from France with a dancing dog; (11) "There are many Princes, but only one Beethoven" "Composers do not cry; composers are made of fire"; (12) Christoph comes to accept Beethoven, Beethoven shows affection for the boy; (13) Beethoven was often beaten by his father and made to practice late; (14) Dishes on floor, papers all over, bed unmade, markings on walls; (15) four bells and a picture made with his own hair; (16) N/A; (17) N/A; (18) N/A; (19) because it is low and dreamy; (20) four.

Beethoven Lives Upstairs

AUDIO: Juno Award Best Children's Recording (Canada), Parents' Choice Silver Honor (U.S.), American Library Association Notable Children's Recording Award, Practical Home Schooling Reader Award Music Curriculum Category and Educational Audio Cassette Category (U.S.), Film Advisory Board Award of Excellence (U.S.), Parents' Choice Classic Award (U.S.), Certified Gold Record (Canada), Certified Platinum Record (Canada)

BOOK: Governor General's Award Finalist – Illustration (Canada), Canadian Children's Book Centre Our Choice Recommendation

VIDEO: Emmy Award for Best Children's Program, Parents' Choice Movie Hall of Fame Classic and Gold Awards (U.S.), Dove Foundation Dove Family Approved Seal, Oppenheim Toy Portfolio Platinum Award (U.S.), Film Advisory Board Award of Excellence (U.S.), Gold Camera Award Best Children's Program and Best Direction (U.S.), Certified Multi-Platinum Video (Canada)

CD-ROM: National Parenting Publications Honors Award (U.S.), Film Advisory Board Award of Excellence (U.S.), Curriculum Administrator Top 100 Districts' Choice Award (U.S.)

Mr. Bach Comes to Call

Parents' Choice Gold Award (U.S.), American Library Association Notable Children's Recording Award, Parents' Choice Classic Award (U.S.), Practical Home Schooling Reader Award Music Curriculum Category and Educational Audio Cassette Category (U.S.), Film Advisory Board Award of Excellence (U.S.), Certified Gold Record (Canada), Certified Platinum Record (Canada)

Tchaikovsky Discovers America

AUDIO: Juno Award Best Children's Recording (Canada), American Library Association Notable Children's Recording Award, Parents' Choice Classic Award (U.S.), Practical Home Schooling Reader Award Music Curriculum Category and Educational Audio Cassette Category (U.S.), Audio File Earphones Award of Excellence (U.S.), Certified Gold Record (Canada)

BOOK: Canadian Children's Book Centre Our Choice Recommendation, Gibbon Award Finalist Illustration (Canada)

Mozart's Magic Fantasy

Juno Award Best Children's Recording (Canada), Parents' Choice Gold Award, American Library Association Notable Children's Recording Award, Parents' Choice Classic Award (U.S.), Practical Home Schooling Reader Award Music Curriculum Category and Educational Audio Cassette Category (U.S.), Film Advisory Board Award of Excellence (U.S.), Certified Gold Record (Canada), Certified Platinum Record (Canada)

Vivaldi's Ring of Mystery

Juno Award Best Children's Recording (Canada), Parent's Choice Gold Award (U.S.), American Library Association Notable Children's Recording Award, Parents' Choice Classic Award (U.S.), Practical Home Schooling Reader Award Music Curriculum Category and Educational Audio Cassette Category (U.S.), Audio File Earphones Award of Excellence (U.S.), Film Advisory Board Award of Excellence (U.S.), Certified Gold Recording (Canada)

Daydreams & Lullabies

Film Advisory Board Award of Excellence (U.S.), Practical Home Schooling Reader Award Music Curriculum Category and Educational Audio Cassette Category (U.S.)

Hallelujah Handel!

Parent's Choice Gold Award (U.S.), Film Advisory Board Award of Excellence (U.S.), Practical Home Schooling Reader Award Music Curriculum Category and Educational Audio Cassette Category (U.S.)

Educational Awards

Curriculum Administrator Top 100 Districts' Choice Award, Learning Magazine – Teacher's Choice Award, Practical Home Schooling Association Notable Children's Recordings

The Classroom Collection

Teacher's Choice Award Learning Magazine

Susan Hammond, Classical Kids Producer

The Order of Canada for her contribution to arts and education in Canada